T0087318

IGOR STRAVINSKY

L'HISTOIRE DU SOLDAT

To access audio visit:
www.halleonard.com/mylibrary

"Enter Code"
4335-6127-1542-9979

ISBN 978-1-59615-450-6

EXCLUSIVELY DISTRIBUTED BY

HAL•LEONARD®

Visit Hal Leonard Online at
www.halleonard.com

Contact Us:
Hal Leonard
7777 West Bluemound Road
Milwaukee, WI 53213
Email: info@halleonard.com

In Europe contact:
Hal Leonard Europe Limited
Distribution Centre, Newmarket Road
Bury St Edmunds, Suffolk, IP33 3YB
Email: info@halleonardeurope.com

In Australia contact:
Hal Leonard Australia Pty. Ltd.
4 Lentara Court
Cheltenham, Victoria, 3192 Australia
Email: info@halleonard.com.au

Contents

L'Histoire du Soldat

The Soldier's March

Stravinsky

4 taps (2 meas.) precede music.

4

Soldier At The Brook

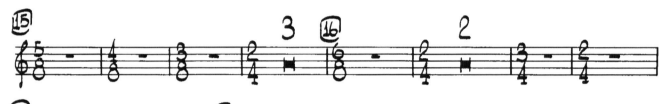

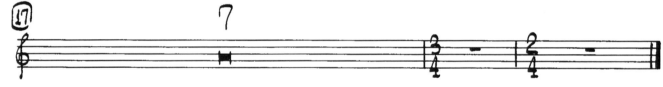

Pastorale

5

The Royal March

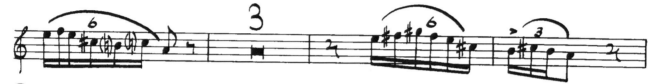

Leggierissimo

mf cantabile

(V.S.)

8

sub. ppp

f (mais moins fort que les bois)

sub. meno f

3

mf

(Solo)

2

sf mais moins fort que les bois

The Little Concert

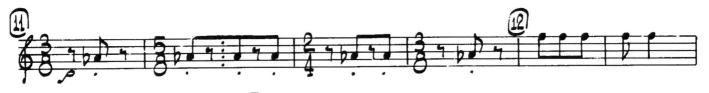

(V.S.)

12

Three Dances
Tango (TACET)

Waltz

Ragtime

The Devil's Dance

4 taps (1 meas.) precede music.

(V.S.)

Grand Chorale

Triumphal March Of The Devil

MORE GREAT BRASS PUBLICATIONS FROM

ᴹᴹᴼ Music Minus One

ADVANCED FRENCH HORN SOLOS, VOL. I

Virtuoso hornist Myron Bloom of the Cleveland Symphony performs these great advanced-level solos on french horn. Then you step in to master this challenging collection! Includes a high-quality printed music score containing the solo part, annotated with performance suggestions; and a compact disc with complete versions (with soloist) followed by piano accompaniments to each piece, minus the soloist.
Performed by Myron Bloom, French horn
Accompaniment: Harriet Wingreen, piano
00400394 Book/CD Pack $14.99

ADVANCED FRENCH HORN SOLOS – VOL. 2

This second volume of advanced solos with piano accompaniment features Dale Clevenger of the Cleveland Symphony playing each of these solos on french horn. Then you take his place with the professional accompanist. Includes a high-quality printed music score containing the solo part, annotated with performance suggestions; and a compact disc with complete versions (with soloist) followed by piano accompaniments to each piece, minus the soloist. Includes: Hindemith, Paul – Sonate in F major: I. Mässig bewegt • Mozart, Wolfgang Amadeus – Horn Concerto No. 4 in E-flat major, KV495: III. Rondo • Strauss, Richard – Horn Concerto No. 1 in E-flat major, op. 11: Rondo.
Performed by Dale Clevenger, French horn
Accompaniment: Meg Bachman Vas, piano
00400676 Book/CD Pack $14.99

BAND AIDS FOR FRENCH HORN

From Bach to Dvořák, this collection of classics arranged presents a unique treat, spanning 200 years of great music, arranged for French Horn and concert band. Includes a high-quality printed music score and a compact disc containing a complete performance with soloist; then a second version with the orchestral accompaniment, minus the soloist.
Performed by Lisa Pike, french horn
Accompaniment: Stuttgart Festival Orchestra
Conductor: Emil Kahn
00400399 Book/CD Pack $14.99

MOZART – TWELVE DUETS FOR TWO FRENCH HORNS

This marvelous group of pieces for two horns is one of Mozart's most wonderful achievements, and a treasure for hornists everywhere. Great music in the classical master's inimitable style. Includes a high-quality printed music score featuring both primo and secondo horn parts; and a compact disc with a complete recording, with the secondo horn on the left channel and the primo horn on the right channel, allowing either to be removed; and an additional version in stereo with the secondo horn only as accompaniment.
Performed by M. Falout, french horn
Accompaniment: M. Falout, french horn
00400391 Book/CD Pack $14.99

PACIFIC COAST HORNS – BRASS QUINTETS FOR TUBA, VOL. 3

Pacific Coast Horns returns in this third volume of greats, performed to perfection in a scintillating reference version. Listen, and then you pick up your instrument and take soloist's duties with the ensemble! 12 songs: Alexander's Ragtime Band • Amazing Grace • Blue Danube • Caravan • Harlem Nocturne • Stompin' at the Savoy • and more.
Featuring Charlie Warren, Tuba with the Pacific Coast Horns Ensemble
00400793 Book/2-CD Pack $14.99

PACIFIC COAST HORNS – MODERN TRUMPET SOLOS WITH BRASS QUINTET, VOL. 3

Kurt Curtis, 1st Trumpet with the Pacific Coast Horns Ensemble
Pacific Coast Horns returns in this third volume of greats, performed to perfection in a scintillating reference version. Listen, and then you pick up your instrument and take soloist's duties with the ensemble! 12 songs: Alexander's Ragtime Band • Amazing Grace • Blue Danube • Caravan • Harlem Nocturne • Stompin' at the Savoy • and more.
Featuring Kurt Curtis, 1st Trumpet with the Pacific Coast Horns Ensemble
00400787 Book/2-CD Pack $14.99

PACIFIC COAST HORNS, VOLUME 1 – TAKE FIVE

(B.C. in C)
Charlie Warren, tuba; Kurt Curtis, 1st trumpet; Evan Avery, 2nd trumpet; Ted Weed, trombone; Mitch Mocilnikar, french horn
Songs: Barber of Seville Overture • In the Dark • Big Band Montage II (Woodchopper's Ball; Cherry Pink and Apple Blossom White; Begin the Beguine; Opus One; Dream) • I Wanna Be like You • Operatic Rag • When the Saints Go Marching In • Bugler's Holiday • Lakme • Flower Duet • Take Five.
Performed by Charlie Warren
00400664 Book/2-CD Set $19.99

HAL•LEONARD®
TRUMPET
PLAY-ALONG

The Trumpet Play-Along Series will help you play your favorite songs quickly and easily. Just follow the printed music, listen to the sound-alike recordings and hear how the trumpet should sound, and then play along using the separate backing tracks.

1. POPULAR HITS

Copacabana (At the Copa) (Barry Manilow) • Does Anybody Really Know What Time It Is? (Chicago) • Hot Hot Hot (Buster Poindexter) • Livin' La Vida Loca (Ricky Martin) • Ring of Fire (Johnny Cash) • Sir Duke (Stevie Wonder) • Sussudio (Phil Collins) • Will It Go Round in Circles (Billy Preston).

00137383 Book/Online Audio $16.99

2. TRUMPET CLASSICS

Ciribiribin (Harry James) • Feels So Good (Chuck Mangione) • Java (Al Hirt) • Music to Watch Girls By (Bob Crewe Generation) • Spanish Flea (Herb Alpert) • Sugar Blues (Al Hirt) • A Taste of Honey (Herb Alpert) • The Toy Trumpet (Raymond Scott).

00137384 Book/Online Audio $16.99

3. CLASSIC ROCK

All You Need Is Love (The Beatles) • Deacon Blues (Steely Dan) • Feelin' Stronger Every Day (Chicago) • Higher Love (Steve Winwood) • September (Earth, Wind & Fire) • Spinning Wheel (Blood, Sweat & Tears) • 25 or 6 to 4 (Chicago) • Vehicle (Ides of March).

00137385 Book/Online Audio $16.99

4. GREAT THEMES

Cherry Pink and Apple Blossom White (Perez Prado) • Deborah's Theme (Ennio Morricone) • Dragnet (Walter Schumann) • The Godfather Waltz (Nino Rota) • Gonna Fly Now (Bill Conti) • Green Hornet Theme (Al Hirt) • The Odd Couple (Neal Hefti) • Sugar Lips (Al Hirt).

00137386 Book/Online Audio $16.99

6. MILES DAVIS

Airegin • Bye Bye Blackbird • Doxy • E.S.P. • Half Nelson • Move • So What • Summertime.

00137447 Book/Online Audio $16.99

7. JAZZ BALLADS

Body and Soul • Easy Living • Everything Happens to Me • I Remember Clifford • Over the Rainbow • Stella by Starlight • They Can't Take That Away from Me • Where or When.

00137475 Book/Online Audio $16.99

HAL•LEONARD®

www.halleonard.com

Prices, contents, and availability subject to change without notice.

1217